HOLD YOUR HEAD HIGH, Butterfly

HOLD YOUR HEAD
HIGH,
Butterfly

WRITTEN AND ILLUSTRATED BY
LINDSEY VANDIVER-SICKLES

For Everett and Ellie
May you see yourselves the way I see you.
May you feel the love I feel for you.

HEY THERE, BUTTERFLY.

So, you busted out of your cocoon.
Super.
I hate to break it to you though—the hard part is still ahead.
So, you'd better listen up, Butterfly. You're gonna need a little
bit of wisdom to get you through.

HOLD YOUR HEAD HIGH, BUTTERFLY.

No one is cooler than you.
Trust me.
Oh, but you're gonna meet
people who think they are.
And let me tell you—those people
are some real stinkers.
They can be mean, poke fun,
or turn up their noses at you.
But stay ABOVE the fray and wait it out.
Someday
they'll see—
the joke's
really on
them.

IT'S OK TO FEEL SHY, BUTTERFLY.

Let's face it—
sometimes you don't
feel like talking; you'd
rather listen instead.
And that's totally rad.
But if you're scared to
speak up or afraid to
show the "real you,"
then snap out of it!
You're cool,
remember?
And you have
AWESOME
things to say.

ALWAYS SAY HI, BUTTERFLY.

Remember how I said it's ok if you don't feel like talking?
Well, that's still true. But at least say hi!
Don't be too big for your britches.
I mean, how would that look—walking around in teeny tiny britches?
And especially don't act ugly to people.
Getting giggles at their expense is not cool at all.
Be **KIND** to everybody—and I do mean everybody.

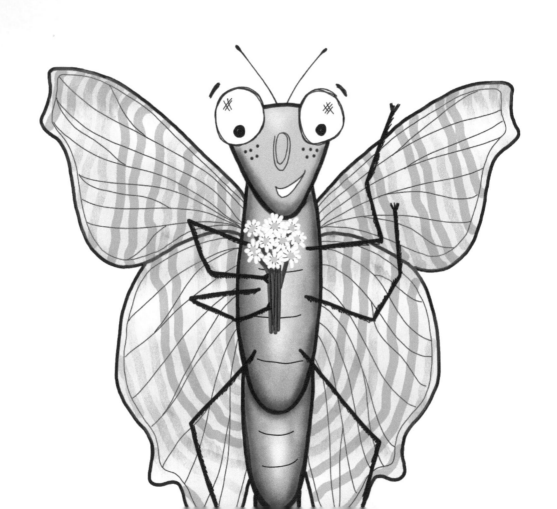

ALWAYS HUG
BEFORE A
GOODBYE,
BUTTERFLY.

So, the point here is that
you don't wanna miss a
chance to show someone
you LOVE 'em.
Plus, hugs just make us feel good.
And when one of your favorite
people says, "I love you," just say,
"I love you more."

KEEP ASKING WHY, BUTTERFLY.

Yeah, you're smart. You know it; I know it.
But don't rest on that.
Be CURIOUS about stuff—wonder why, wonder how.
Never stop discovering.

DON'T TELL THAT BIG LIE, BUTTERFLY.

Mmm hmm—I see what you're doing. You messed up and now you're trying to cover it up. Well, you see, messing up is ok. We ALL do it. But just like you gotta LEARN new things, you've also gotta learn from those mistakes.

ALWAYS, ALWAYS TRY, BUTTERFLY.

Nobody said it was gonna be easy.
I mean, sometimes it feels downright impossible.
But you, my friend, are **FIERCE**.
You are relentless.

You will break through the thickest of walls, climb the highest of heights, weather the stormiest of storms...
Ok, you get the idea:
Be persistent.

SAVOR THAT TASTY PIE, BUTTERFLY.

All that persistence is hard work, and you sure can't shy away from a little elbow grease. But don't forget to take time to enjoy life too. Some say to "stop and smell the roses," but I prefer eating pie. In fact, my two favorite kinds of pie are hot pie and cold pie. And you can't go wrong with chocolate. *OOOH*, but fruit pies are good too. Also, the point I was making before I started thinking about pie—do that too.

IT'S OK TO CRY, BUTTERFLY.

No one is too big,
or too small,
or too important,
or too brave to cry.
Letting it all out
sure does make us
feel better.
Plus, if you bottle it
up, you might actually
explode. *BOOM!*
And that just sounds
messy.

TAKE A MOMENT TO SIGH, BUTTERFLY.

What's another way to avoid exploding? Deep breaths. Taking just a few seconds to sit quietly. And if that sounds boring, just pretend you're a dragon. And every time you breathe, FIRE comes out. I mean, how cool would that be?!

LOOK TO THE SKY, BUTTERFLY.

"What's in the sky," you ask?
Well, really, it's the One who's also everywhere else.
And that's God.
He loves you and guides you and takes care of you.
And yes, He still lets bad things happen to you sometimes.
But He will also give you **PEACE** in the middle of the biggest
storm. You've gotta be patient, though. Sometimes He makes
you wait for things—loooong waits—like when you've been in
the car for F O R E V E R.

KEEP YOUR FAMILY CLOSE BY, BUTTERFLY.

You see, God gives us these real-life **ANGEL** people, except sometimes these angels might really seem like devils. They'll fight with you; they'll punish you; they'll annoy you. But they'll see YOUR ugly side too. They'll know all the worst things about you, and they'll still love you. Come what may, they'll stick by you and lift you up.

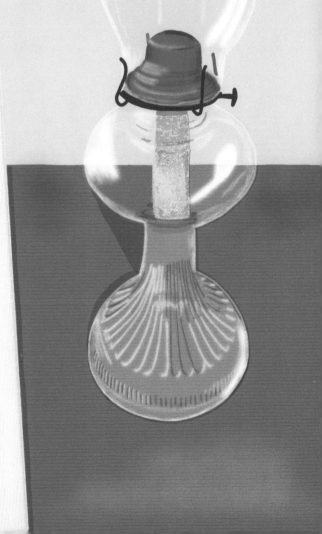

OK, BUTTERFLY.

I get it. That's enough advice. Now turn around and take a leap.

Keep these words in your head
and in your heart,
and you will

fly,

BUTTERFLY!

CPSIA information can be obtained
at www.ICGtesting.com
Printed in the USA
BVHW061332041121
620396BV00002B/11